THE NEW ME

Sharna Jackson

Illustrated by **Aaron Cushley**

OXFORD
UNIVERSITY PRESS

> Letter from the Author

Hello! I'm Sharna Jackson, the author of *The New Me*. Like Dean in this story, I'm always trying to find different things to do. This means I've had lots of different jobs. I've worked in many museums and galleries, with book publishers – I even made an app once.

As well as writing this book, I have also written books about art, and mystery stories like *High Rise Mystery*. I also wrote a book with 1281 kids called *London/Londoff* which was so much fun.

I was born and raised in a town called Luton, lived in London for ages and I've just moved to Rotterdam to live on my old ship called *Anna Maria* with my son Joseph and his dad.

Sharna Jackson

Kezia shook the test tube in her hand. The liquid inside turned from green to red.

'Cool!' she said.

'Not cool,' I snorted.

Dad sighed.

'What's wrong with you, Dean?' said Kezia. 'You're being annoying!'

'You're annoying! You're the worst sister – why are you always doing experiments?' I asked.

'You know I love science. It's my thing,' said Kezia.

'Your thing? What's *my* thing?' I asked.

'Being rude?' said Kezia.
I sighed. 'I want a *thing*.'
'You like *lots* of things,' said Dad.
'Reading, being outside, nice food—'

'Everyone likes nice food, Dad,' I said. 'That's not special. I want my own thing!'

'You don't need one; you're great as you are,' replied Dad.

'When you're not being grumpy,' said Kezia. 'Wait, I've got an idea!' She took a letter out of her bag. 'You could sign up for a club at school.'

'Perfect!' I said. I peered at the long list of clubs. There was everything – from cooking to craft, and football to French.

'So, which one?' asked Dad.
'All of them,' I said.
Dad laughed. 'Choose three, Dean – that's a good number.'

'OK.' I closed my eyes and jabbed my finger at the form. 'My first choice is ... ' I opened my right eye. 'Coding Club. Exciting!' I tapped on the paper twice and opened both eyes. 'Then it's Art Club and Yoga.'

I sat back in my chair and grinned at my family.

'I hope you're ready for the new me!' I told them.

* * *

As I walked to the computer room at lunchtime on Monday, I thought about Coding Club. Apps, websites, games – it would be awesome.

Coding will definitely be my thing!

I opened the door.
Laptops. Everywhere.
I took a deep breath.
'Hello!' said Ms Hunter. 'We're learning how to make characters jump today.'
Coding Club was *exactly* how I'd imagined.
This was the new me!

CODING CLUB

I sat down and grabbed the mouse.
I tried following the instructions, but
my character barely left the ground.

This was harder than I thought.

Ms Hunter leaned over. 'Nice work.
Can you make her jump higher?'

I could do it. I knew I could.
This was the new me, after all.

I stared at the screen. I typed, I dragged, I dropped.

My character jumped higher – but then she wouldn't stop.

I tried everything, but she bounced and bounced – right off the screen! I couldn't get her back.

I slumped in my chair.
Coding wasn't *my* thing.
This wasn't the new me.

* * *

As I skipped to the Art room on Wednesday, I thought about Art Club. Painting, pastels, photography – it would be awesome.

Art will definitely be my thing!

I opened the door.
Paint. Everywhere.
I took a deep breath.
'Hi!' said Mr Anthony. 'We're working on self-portraits today.'
Art Club was *exactly* how I'd imagined. This was the new me!

I sat down and grabbed a paintbrush. I looked at my face in the mirror and started painting, but my portrait looked nothing like it was supposed to.

This was harder than it looked.

'Great start – now focus on your eyes,' said Mr Anthony.

I could do it. I knew I could. This was the new me, after all.

I stared at my painting. I reached over for a clean brush – but I knocked my water pot over. My picture was ruined.

I sighed.

Art wasn't *my* thing, either.

This wasn't the new me.

* * *

As I ran to the hall at lunchtime on Friday, I thought about Yoga Club.

YOGA CLUB

Yoga will *definitely* be my thing! Third time lucky.

I opened the door.
Yoga mats. Everywhere.
I took a deep breath.

'Welcome!' said Mr Chan. 'We're focusing on our breathing today.'

Yoga Club was *exactly* how I'd imagined.

This was the new me!

21

I lay down and stared at the ceiling. I could do this. I knew how to breathe, after all.

Mr Chan smiled at me. 'That's exactly right. In through your nose, out through your mouth,' he said.

I was doing it. I knew I could.
This was the new me after all.
I thought about Coding, and Art.
I could try them again. It didn't matter that they didn't work out.
I began to relax.

As I lay there, I realized something.
I was proud that I'd tried.
That was me.
'Are you ready to begin?' asked Mr Chan.
I was ready.
Yoga was my thing – but not my *only* thing.
Just being *me* was my thing.